Easy Classical Melodica Solos

Easy Classical Melodica Solos

Arranged and edited by JAVIER MARCÓ

Easy Classical Melodica Solos
© 2011 by Javier Marcó. All Rights Reserved. International Copyright Secured.
© 2011 Cover Photographs by Eugenia Pereyra. All Rights Reserved.

ISBN-13:978-1463776954
ISBN-10:1463776950

Unauthorized reproduction of any part of this publication by any means including photocopying is an infringement of copyright.

Contents

Playing guide 7

1812 Overture 13

A Little Night Music 14

The Blue Danube 15

Bridal Chorus 16

Dance of the Flowers 17

Für Elise 18

Greensleeves 19

Jesu, Joy of Man Desiring 20

La Donna é Mobile 21

Land of Hope and Glory 22

Lullaby 23

Minuet in G 24

Ode to Joy 25

Spring - Four Seasons 26

Water Music 28

Playing guide

Standard notation
Notes are written on a Staff.

Staff
The staff consists of five lines and four spaces, on which notes symbols are placed.

Clef
A clef assigns an individual note to a certain line.
The **Treble Clef** or **G Clef** is used for the Melodica.

This clef indicates the position of the note G which is on the second line from the bottom.

Note
A note is a sign used to represent the relative pitch of a sound. There are seven notes: A, B, C, D, E, F and G.

Ledger lines
The ledger lines are used to inscribe notes outside the lines and spaces of the staff.

Accidentals
An accidental is a symbol to raise or lower the pitch of a note.

♯ sharp   Next note up half step.

♭ flat   Next note down half step.

♮ natural   Cancels a flat or a sharp.

Note values

A **note value** is used to indicate the duration of a note. A **rest** is an interval of silence, marked by a sign indicating the length of the pause. Each rest corresponds to a particular note value.

𝅝	Whole note	𝄻	Whole rest
𝅗𝅥	Half note	𝄼	Half rest
𝅘𝅥	Quarter note	𝄽	Quarter rest
𝅘𝅥𝅮	Eighth note	𝄾	Eighth rest
𝅘𝅥𝅯	Sixteenth note	𝄿	Sixteenth rest

Dotted note

A dotted note is a note with a small dot written after it. The dot adds half as much again to the basic note's duration.

Tie

A tie is a curved line connecting the heads of two notes of the same pitch, indicating that they are to be played as a single note with a duration equal to the sum of the individual notes' note values.

Bars or Measures

The staff is divided into equal segments of time consisting of the same number of beats, called bar or measures.

Measure   Measure   Measure   Measure

↑
Bar line

Time signature

Time signature consists of two numbers, the upper number specifies how many beats (or counts) are in each measure, and the lower number tells us the note value which represents one beat.

one   two   three   four

Example: 4/4 means four quarters, or four beats per measure with a quarter note receiving one beat or count.

Key signature

A Key signature is a group of accidentals, generally written at the beginning of a score immediately after the clef, and shows which notes always get sharps or flats. Accidentals on the lines and spaces in the key signature affect those notes throughout the piece unless there is a natural sign.

Repeat sign

The repeat sign indicates a section should be repeated from the beginning, and then continue on. A corresponding sign facing the other way indicates where the repeat is to begin.

↑ Repeat Sign

First and second endings

The section should be repeated from the beginning, and number brackets above the bars indicate which to played the first time (1), which to play the second time (2).

Fingering

In this book right hand fingering is indicated using numbers above the staff, and left hand fingering is indicated using numbers below the staff.

1= thumb
2= index
3= middle
4= ring
5= little finger

Dynamics

Dynamics refers to the volume of the notes.

p   (piano), meaning soft.
mp   (mezzo-piano), meaning "moderately soft".
mf   (mezzo-forte), meaning "moderately loud".
f   (forte), meaning loud.

———— **Crescendo**. A gradual increase in volume.

———— **Decrescendo**. A gradual decrease in volume.

Tempo Markings
Tempo is written at the beginning of a piece of music and indicates how slow or fast this piece should be played.

Lento — very slow (40–60 bpm)
Adagio — slow and stately (66–76 bpm)
Andate — at a walking pace (76–108 bpm)
Moderato — moderately (101-110 bpm)
Allegro — fast, quickly and bright (120–139 bpm)
Allegretto — moderately fast (but less so than allegro)
Alla marcia — in the manner of a march
In tempo di valse — in tempo of vals

rallentando — gradual slowing down
a tempo — returns to the base tempo after a *rallentando*

Articulation

Legato. Notes are played smoothly and connected.

Stacatto. Notes are played separated or detached from its neighbours by a silence.

Fermata (pause)
The note is to be prolonged at the pleasure of the performer.

1812 Overture

Pyotr Ilyich Tchaikovsky
Arr. by Javier Marcó

Alla Marcia

A Little Night Music

Wolfgang Amadeus Mozart
Arr. by Javier Marcó

Allegro

The Blue Danube

Johann Strauss
Arr. by Javier Marcó

Tempo di valse

Bridal Chorus

Richard Wagner
Arr. by Javier Marcó

Allegro

mf

Dance of the Flowers

Pyotr Ilyich Tchaikovsky
Arr. by Javier Marcó

Tempo di valse

mf

Für Elise

Ludwig Van Beethoven
Arr. by Javier Marcó

Greensleves

Anonymous
Arr. by Javier Marcó

Moderato

mf

Jesu, Joy of Man Desiring

Johann Sebastian Bach
Arr. by Javier Marcó

La Donna è Mobile

Giuseppe Verdi
Arr. by Javier Marcó

Allegro

Land Of Hope And Glory

Edward Elgar
Arr. by Javier Marcó

Alla marcia, maestoso

Lullaby

Johannes Brahms
Arr. by Javier Marcó

Adagio

Minuet in G

Johann Sebastian Bach
Arr. by Javier Marcó

Ode to Joy

Ludwig Van Beethoven
Arr. by Javier Marcó

Spring - Four Seasons

Antonio Vivaldi
Arr. by Javier Marcó

Allegro

Water Music

George Frideric Handel
Arr. by Javier Marcó

Alle Hornpipe

info@marcomusica.com

Printed in Poland
by Amazon Fulfillment
Poland Sp. z o.o., Wrocław